Getting To Know...

# Nature's Children

## OSTRICHES

Merebeth Switzer

GROLIER
BOOKS

## FACTS IN BRIEF

**Classification of the Ostrich**

    Class:    *Aves* (birds)
    Order:    *Struthioniformes* (ostrich)
    Family:   *Struthionidae*
    Genus:   *Struthio*
    Species: *Struthio camelus*

**World distribution.**   Africa.

**Habitat.**   Plains and deserts.

**Distinctive physical characteristics.**   The largest living bird, and the only one with two toes. Has long, featherless legs, a long neck and a small head. Body is covered in loose, soft feathers. Male is black with white wing and tail feathers. Female is a dull brown color.

**Habits.**   Ostriches cannot fly but are excellent runners. They live in large groups made up of families that consist of one male and several hens. Defend themselves with their powerful legs.

**Diet.**   Vegetation, insects and occasionally small animals.

This series is approved and recommended by the Federation of Ontario Naturalists.

Grolier Books is a division of Grolier Enterprises, Inc.
All rights reserved.
ISBN: 0-7172-6493-9

GROLIER
BOOKS

90 Sherman Turnpike, Danbury, Connecticut 06816

## Have you ever wondered . . .

Which bird weighs almost as much as two adults, stands taller than a professional basketball player and has feathers that have been prized by kings and emperors for thousands of years? It is the ostrich. This amazing creature is the largest bird in the world today, and it is one of a kind.

Keep reading to find out more about this unusual bird and its life in the wild.

## Beating the Heat

It is a hot, sunny day in southern Africa. Herds of gnus, gazelles and zebras graze in the tall grass. Looking out over the crowd are three small, flat heads perched on long, naked necks. Ostriches!

Two of the ostriches have dull, brown feathers. These are the females, or hens. The third ostrich, the largest one, has black feathers and a feathery white rump. He is the male, or cock. Gathered around his ankles are several speckled chicks who are using him as a sun umbrella. If there are no trees nearby to provide shade, young ostriches depend on their parents to shield them from the tropical sun.

*By the time these baby ostriches are six months old they will be as big as their father.*

# One of a Kind

Ostrich relatives walked the Earth over 50 million years ago. Today, however, the ostrich is the only one of its kind. It has no living relatives.

Unlike the skeletons of dinosaurs and ancient mammals, those of most birds are very fragile and easily broken. There are therefore few fossils and bones to tell us about the ostrich's ancestors. The only thing we know for certain is that of the seven types of ostriches that once lived, six have disappeared during the last million years.

And the seventh nearly disappeared too. Ostriches used to live in Europe, Asia and Africa. Then, in the 1800s, their beautiful feathers became so popular as decorations for hats and clothing that wild ostriches were in danger of becoming extinct. By 1900, they could be found only in parts of Africa. Fortunately, styles changed and ostrich feathers were no longer in demand.

*The ostrich is also known as the
"camel bird."*

*Some ostriches may live to be 70 years old.*

## Ostrich Country

Ostriches tend to live in open areas where there are few trees or shrubs.

Just as people differ from country to country, so ostriches that live in one area don't look quite the same as those from other areas. Some are larger than others. Some have small tufts of feathers on their heads, while the heads of others are almost naked. In some areas, the skin on the ostriches' legs and neck is a reddish color, while in other regions it is bluish-gray.

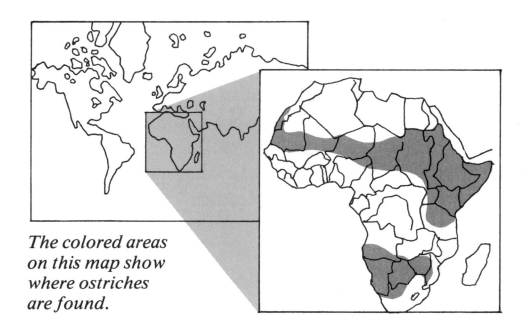

*The colored areas on this map show where ostriches are found.*

10

# Do All Birds Fly?

When we think of birds we usually think of them flying. But not all birds fly. Penguins, for example, are excellent swimmers, while ostriches are superb runners. Although penguins and ostriches cannot fly, they have two things in common with all other birds: they have feathers and they lay eggs.

Did ostriches ever fly? Some scientists think they did, but that at some point the birds lost this ability. Why? Perhaps they lived in an area where there were few enemies and a food supply was not far away. Ancient ostriches would then have had no need to fly and their bodies would gradually have changed until eventually they could no longer do so.

Other experts believe that ostriches never flew. They argue that birds that can fly have hollow, lightweight bones and can easily get off the ground. Ostriches have solid, heavy bones. This alone would prevent a giant bird from being able to fly.

## Fastest on Land

Whether it once flew or not, flying is not important to the modern ostrich which is the fastest bird on dry land. At full speed, not only could it zip right past a car driving down a city street, but it can run faster than many birds can fly. An ostrich can also outrun most other animals, and unlike them, it can keep up its speed for 15 to 20 minutes. Although the cheetah is faster, it cannot sustain its speed for more than a few seconds, or 400 metres (1/4 mile).

## Karate Kicks

The ostrich is an efficient running machine. While most birds have three or four toes, the ostrich is the only bird with just two. Its toes have grown together to form a foot which is as strong as a horse's hoof. This helps the ostrich cover long distances at high speeds, while its wide feet keep the ostrich from sinking into the sand as it runs. And if you look at the size of its muscular thighs, you will see where the ostrich gets the power to keep running.

The ostrich's legs are important for more than just getting around, however. Although ostriches prefer to run from danger, if they are ever cornered by an enemy they will lash out with a deadly karate kick that can kill a lion. And their sharp toenails can slash anything in their path.

*An ostrich's big toe may be 18 centimetres (7 inches) long.*

# Burying its Head in the Sand

A well-known fable about the ostrich describes the bird burying its head in the sand when it is frightened. The story is just not true. Any ostrich that tried this would almost certainly smother.

So where did the story come from? Probably from the fact that nesting ostriches sometimes stretch their neck out along the ground. No one knows for sure why an ostrich does this, but some people think that it may be trying to fool enemies into mistaking its feathery rump for a shrub. Of course this trick only works if the ostrich is nesting among vegetation and not on open sand.

*To make herself and her nest more difficult to spot, the female ostrich will sometimes stretch her neck along the ground and hope her body looks like a brown bush.*

## What's for Dinner?

Ostriches eat seeds, fruit, vines, leaves and the shoots of new plants. They even eat the African version of the thorny cactus. And if an insect, a lizard or even a small mouse walks by, the ostrich is quick to gobble up the meaty snack. Although ostriches prefer plants, they will eat just about anything. They cannot be very choosy about food, especially during droughts or other times when food is scarce.

Ostriches swallow bits of stone and grit with their meals. Why? Because they have no teeth, they cannot chew their food. The gravel they swallow grinds things up in the gizzard so food can be digested more easily.

## Keeping Clean

Some people think that the ostrich can live without water, but this is not true. The ostrich gets some water from its food but it needs drinking water and it makes frequent visits to waterholes. While there, it often takes time out for a bath, sitting right down in the pond and splashing water over its body with its wings.

Like many smaller birds, the ostrich also takes dust baths. It throws sand over itself and works it through its dry feathers with its beak. The sand removes small mites and lice and bits of oil and dirt from the ostrich's body.

To save water, the ostrich will try to stand in the shade during the hottest part of the day. If there are no trees nearby, it will stand facing the sun with its wings outstretched to shade its body. Standing in this position leaves its flanks open to the air. They serve as the ostrich's "radiator" by releasing extra heat.

*Ostriches like water and bathe whenever they can.*

## Long Lashes and Safety Goggles

Ostriches have long black eyelashes which are beautiful *and* useful—they protect the ostrich's eyes from sand and dirt carried by the wind. Unlike your eyelashes, which are small hairs, an ostrich's eyelashes are made of very narrow feathers. Like all birds, the ostrich has no hair on its body—only feathers.

The ostrich also has a built-in pair of safety goggles. It has a top and bottom eyelid, just like you do, but it also has a third, see-through eyelid. When needed, this lid slides across the eye to give it extra protection.

*Note the feathered eyelashes of this ostrich.*

## Help from Above

An ostrich is so tall it would bump its head if it went through the front door of your house. Being this tall makes the ostrich a super lookout tower. And with eyes the size of tennis balls, it can see things that are very far away. Ostriches are able to give plenty of warning of approaching danger. This talent makes them valuable neighbors to animals such as zebras and antelopes which have limited vision.

But zebras and antelopes can also help the ostrich. How? They have a keener sense of smell and can pick up the odor of any intruder that the ostrich does not spot, especially at night. Not only that, their hooves stir up extra insects—a tasty treat for the ostrich.

*A head above the rest.*

## Family Life

Ostriches live in large groups made up of small families. During the fall breeding and hatching season, each family goes off by itself. In a family there is usually only one male, who will have three to five hens as his mates.

Like many male birds, the cock works to attract the attention of the hens when it is time to mate. An ostrich has a very loud booming call that some people say resembles a lion's roar. By gulping air into its throat and then letting it out quickly, the ostrich makes an impressive *boo-boo-BOOO-hoo* that carries for great distances. The cock uses this sound to attract a hen. She shows her interest by answering him with the same call.

*When running at full speed an ostrich takes giant strides up to 5 metres (16 feet) long.*

## Let's Dance!

If the hen responds to the male, a spectacular mating dance begins. The birds run around each other and flap their billowy wings. Then the hen squats on the ground and rocks from side to side, flapping her wings. The two birds caress each other with their necks and exchange calls and gentle bites.

Suddenly the female jumps up and runs off across the open plain. The male follows and when he catches up, he struts around her, fluffing out his tail and body feathers like a peacock. If the hen is still interested in the male, mating takes place. If she isn't, the dance may continue until she changes her mind or the male gives up.

*Strutting his stuff.*

## Shared Responsibilities

Mating takes place towards the end of the dry season, before the rains begin. This is nature's way of making sure that the eggs do not get too wet to hatch. It also means that the chicks hatch in the rainy season, a time when food is easily available. That is important for ostriches with a family to feed.

Ostrich hens from the same family often share the same nest, a shallow pit that the male has hollowed out in the sandy soil. Each female lays one cream-colored egg every other day until she has deposited about six to eight eggs in the nest. One nest may contain up to 60 eggs!

The male is never far away during the two weeks when the eggs are laid.

*The hen blends in well with the chosen nesting site.*

# Extra Large Eggs

It makes sense that the ostrich, the largest bird in the world, lays the largest egg in the world. The average egg is about the size of a cantaloupe and weighs about 1.5 kilograms (3 pounds). That's quite an egg! In fact, an ostrich egg equals 24 chicken's eggs.

The cock takes on much of the responsibility of caring for the eggs by sitting on them to keep them warm throughout the night. His black feathers make him difficult to see in the dark. The females take turns sitting on the eggs during the day when their sandy colored feathers blend in with their surroundings, making them less visible to enemies. Sometimes one of the females will drive the weaker females away from the nest, and she and her mate take over the care of all the eggs.

*Keeping watch.*

## Protecting the Nest

No matter who is sitting on the eggs, one of the other adults is always nearby. A full-grown ostrich has few enemies, but eggs and chicks can fall prey to jackals, hyenas, lions, cheetahs, hawks and eagles.

Sometimes one of the adults, usually the male, will lure intruders away by pretending to be injured. He looks like an easy target as he shuffles awkwardly along the ground as if he's in pain. Before the hungry predator realizes what is happening, it has been led away from the eggs by a suddenly very healthy and very fast adult ostrich.

If the wounded bird trick doesn't work, the ostrich will charge at the predator, screaming.

*"Don't come any closer!"*

# Here They Come

Inside the eggs the chicks are developing. They grow quickly as their bodies absorb the nutritious yolk. Several times each day their parents turn the eggs. This prevents the growing chick from sticking to the sides of the shell and lets its body develop evenly all over.

The chick's body continues to grow inside the egg until there is nowhere to go but out. About six weeks after the eggs are laid, the chicks begin to hatch. The sound of a hatching chick can sometimes be so loud that it may cause the startled parent to jump up off the nest in surprise!

One by one, the chicks peck their way through the eggshell. Since the shell is as thick as a dinner plate, hatching takes an hour or more. The chick must do this on its own. Its parents are too big and their beaks are too broad and flat to be of help.

*"Hello, world!"*

## The First Steps

As soon as the chick hatches, it attaches itself to the first living thing it sees, which is usually its parents. The male's legs are a brighter color at this time of year, which makes it easy for the chicks to follow him as they explore the dusty plains.

Baby ostriches are 30 centimetres (a foot) tall when they hatch, and can stand up shortly afterwards. Under the hot sun their feathers dry quickly, and it is not long before they are ready to tag along with the rest of the flock. Their bodies grow quickly, and by running with the adult birds, they develop the strong legs they will need throughout their lives. Of course, it takes the chicks a little while before they can keep up, but by one month of age they can run as fast as their parents.

*Learning to stay perfectly still will keep ostrich chicks safe from their enemies.*

# Special Words

**Camouflage**  Colors and patterns that help an animal blend in with its surroundings.

**Chick**  A young bird before or after hatching.

**Cock**  A male bird.

**Fossil**  Remains (often prehistoric) of a plant or animal that are preserved in the earth.

**Gizzard**  A second stomach in a bird where food is ground up.

**Hatch**  To emerge from an egg.

**Hen**  A female bird.

**Mate**  To come together to produce young. Either member of an animal pair is also the other's mate.

**Predator**  An animal that hunts other animals for food.

**Yolk**  Yellow internal part of an egg that nourishes the chick before it hatches.

# INDEX

**Cover Photo:** Boyd Norton

**Photo Credits:** Ziesler (Peter Arnold/Hot Shots), page 4; Robert Winslow, page 7;
Focus/Reflexion, page 8; Bill Ivy, pages 11, 23, 27, 43; M.P. Kahl (Vireo), pages
14-15, 24, 39; Bob Wavra, page 16; Len Lee Rue III (Photo Researchers), pages 18,
32; P. Davey (Vireo), pages 20, 31; J.D. Taylor, page 28; Len Rue Jr., page 35;
A. Purcell (Words & Pictures), page 36; Zoological Society of San Diego, pages 40,
44; Breck Kent, page 46.

# Getting To Know...

# Nature's Children

# OLD WORLD MONKEYS

## Bill Ivy

GROLIER
BOOKS

# FACTS IN BRIEF

**Classification of Old World Monkeys**

|  |  |
|---|---|
| Class: | *Mammalia* (mammals) |
| Order: | *Primates* (monkeys, apes, lemurs, people) |
| Family: | *Cercopithecidae* |
| Subfamilies: | *Cercopithecinae* (monkeys with cheek pouches) |
| | *Colobinae* (leaf monkeys) |
| Genus: | There are 12 genera of Old World Monkeys. |
| Species: | There are over 70 species of Old World Monkeys. |

**World distribution.**　Africa, India, China, Japan and Southeast Asia.

**Habitat.**　Varies with species.

**Distinctive physical characteristics.**　Most species have arms and legs of equal length, opposable thumbs and big toes, and a long tail. The nostrils are curved, close together and open downwards. There are thick calluses on the buttocks.

**Habits.**　Live in communities of 4 to 100. Most sleep in trees at night. Mainly active during the day.

**Diet.**　Varies with species.

This series is approved and recommended by the Federation of Ontario Naturalists.

Grolier Books is a division of Grolier Enterprises, Inc.
All rights reserved.
ISBN: 0-7172-6493-9

GROLIER
B O O K S

90 Sherman Turnpike, Danbury, Connecticut 06816

# Have you ever wondered . . .

Which animals do you think are the most popular ones at the zoo? Probably the monkeys and for good reason. With their expressive faces and humorous antics they often remind us of mischievous little people. In fact, when people play pranks we may say they are up to "monkey business" and when we are teased by our friends we may tell them to stop "monkeying around."

Monkeys are not only playful, they are curious, noisy, intelligent and they're great acrobats as well. People have always been fascinated by them and in some countries monkeys are considered sacred.

Want to have more fun than a barrel of monkeys? Then turn the page and learn more about these incredible animals.

*Barbary macaque.*

## Old or New

Most monkeys live in the tropics where the weather is always warm but a few live in areas where the winters are very cold. Scientists divide monkeys into two groups. Those that live in Central and South America are called New World monkeys, while those found in Africa and Asia are called Old World monkeys.

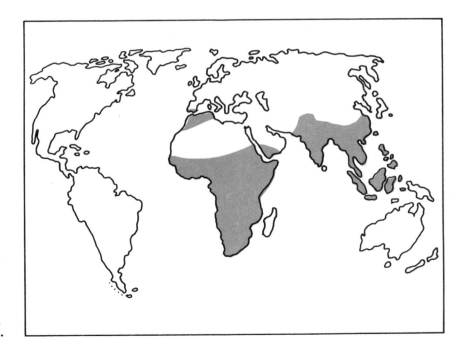

*The shaded areas on this map show where Old World monkeys are found.*

There are several ways to tell which group a particular monkey belongs to even if you don't know where it came from. If the monkey has a prehensile, or grasping, tail and can use it as an extra hand for picking up things or swinging from trees, it is a New World monkey. No Old World monkey can do these things with its tail. You can also tell by looking closely at the monkey's face. Old World monkeys have nostrils that are close together and open towards the front. The nostrils of a New World monkey are wide, round, and further apart, and they open to the sides.

Only Old World monkeys have their own handy seat cushions, pads of tough skin on their bottom to make sitting more comfortable. Some also have cheek pouches for storing food. And many Old World monkeys have something else very special that New World monkeys don't — opposable thumbs just like yours.

*Black-tailed marmoset* *NEW WORLD*

*De Brazza's monkey* *OLD WORLD*

## Thumbs Up

Take a close look at one of your hands and pick something up. Did you notice how you used your thumb and fingers together? Now try it again only this time without using your thumb. Not so easy, is it? We are able to move our thumb around to meet our fingers so we are said to have opposable thumbs.

Many Old World monkeys also have opposable thumbs. But they have something we don't have — opposable big toes! This means they can pick up objects as easily with their feet as they can with their hands. And these special toes and thumbs are very useful for climbing trees, swinging from branch to branch, peeling fruit and just about everything else.

*Macaque hand*

*The hand of the lion-tailed macaque is very similar to your own, nails and all.*

## Real Troopers

Opposite page:
*A troop of olive baboons on the move.*

Monkeys, like apes, lemurs and people, are primates. Old World monkeys are strong, agile animals with long limbs. In fact, their arms are about the same length as their legs, which helps them to be great climbers and also fast runners on all fours. Their tail varies from a mere stub to an elegant plume longer than their body. Their size ranges from the tiny talapoin, which weighs about a kilogram (2.2 pounds), to the mighty baboon, which may tip the scales at 45 kilograms (100 pounds).

Monkeys enjoy each other's company and rarely live alone. Some stay in pairs but most gather in groups known as troops. A troop may contain anywhere from 4 to over 100 individuals. Often one male plus several females and their young make up a troop.

High up in the trees monkeys have few enemies. While an occasional owl or hawk may attack a youngster, their main concern is other primates. However, those species that spend a lot of time on the ground have to be on the lookout for animals such as cheetahs, lions and jackals.

## Monkey Sense

All monkeys are intelligent, but the Old World species are believed to be even brighter than their New World relatives. Apparently they rely less on instinct and more on reason. And they have an excellent memory, remembering from season to season where their favorite trees are and exactly when the fruit will be ripe.

Monkeys have very good eyesight and it's a good thing they do: leaping from branch to branch and being short-sighted could be quite a problem. Many mammals see the world in shades of gray, but monkeys see in color just as we do, and most of them see better in daylight than at night. Their sense of smell is good but not as keen as that of many other animals. They rely on their eyes more than their nose to find food. Since they have such small ears they often have to turn their head from side to side to zero in on sounds.

*The Japanese macacque is known for its inventiveness as well as for its ability to withstand bitterly cold winters.*

## On the Menu

Many people think monkeys live mainly on bananas, but actually they eat an incredible variety of food. Here is a list of some of their favorite things: fruit, nuts, seeds, leaves, tubers, flowers, insects, spiders, crabs and birds' eggs. Some even eat small mammals. Many species live almost entirely on leaves. With their agile hands they have no trouble peeling fruit or removing bark from trees to find the juicy insects underneath. Of course monkeys also need water to live and most drink by drawing in water with their lips. A few, however, lap up water like a dog.

Monkeys must find fresh food each day since they store only what they can hold in their cheeks. Cheek pouches actually extend below the jaws and can pack quite a bit of food — possibly as much as a stomachful for some species.

*One hand for food still leaves one for cuddling the baby. (Vervet monkeys)*

# Chitter Chatter

Monkeys talk to each other but not in words as we do. Instead they use a variety of different sounds, depending on whether they are happy, angry or afraid. Their most common call is a rapid chattering. When they are angry they shriek and scold each other. The loud call of the male rallies the rest of the troop together, warns of danger and lets other groups in the area know where he is and who's in charge.

Because monkeys have such expressive faces it is easy to tell what kind of mood they are in. Whether they are curious, content, happy or excited, you can see it on their faces. When it is angry a monkey pulls back its lips and shows its teeth. When it is tired or bored it lets out a big yawn.

*When a male hamadryas baboon shows his teeth, he **really** has something to show.*

## Grooming Parties

Do you enjoy having your hair washed, dried and brushed? Many people find this relaxing. For monkeys, having their coat groomed is just as enjoyable, and it's helpful too. They spend a lot of time carefully removing dirt and insects from each other's hair, using their hands and often their teeth as well. Social standing in the troop determines who grooms who. Friends of equal status groom each other, while a male leader may have many lower ranking members wanting to groom him. Mothers and other females often groom the young ones.

Monkeys groom each other not only to rid themselves of pests, but often just for fun. In the same way that we like to visit with our friends, monkeys like to get together for a grooming party. It helps to calm them down and is probably a way of showing affection and friendship.

*"Where on earth did you pick this up?" (Mandrills)*

## I'm All Ears

By the time most monkeys are four or five years old they are ready to start a family. Females mate with the leader of the troop to make sure they have the strongest, healthiest father for their offspring. Young males usually have to fight with older males for the chance to mate with females in the troop. Often it takes a male quite some time and many attempts at a number of troops before he wins a mate.

About six months after mating the female gives birth to a single infant — in rare cases twins. She usually has her baby at night high up in a tree. She does not make a nest or prepare any type of nursery. Immediately after birth the wide-eyed and alert youngster clings to the fur on its mother's belly. If it cannot support its own weight the mother will put her hand on its back for extra support. She also gives her baby its first bath by licking it clean.

Except for being able to grab hold, a newborn monkey is totally helpless. It is covered in soft velvety fur which is often a different color than that of its parents.

Opposite page:
*Like most baby monkeys, this young hamadryas baboon has ears that seem way too big for its head.*

21

## Monkey See, Monkey Do

For the first few days of its life the newborn monkey spends its time sleeping and nursing on its mother's milk. It will be at least six months to a year before it will be weaned. In at least one species the baby monkey sucks its thumb.

In some families the father helps to look after his offspring and may even carry it around. Sometimes other members of the troop babysit the youngster. But no matter who is helping out, the mother keeps a watchful eye and ear out for her baby and will return to its side at the least sign of trouble.

By the third month the young monkey's coat is gradually replaced by a new fluffier one which is similar to its parents' fur but not as clearly marked. By this time too, the youngster has begun to learn by copying what its mother does. When mother and child go off looking for food, the young monkey eats the same things it sees her eating. Soon it knows what's good to eat and what isn't.

*This baby silvered langur's spectacular orange coat will last only a few months.*

# Monkeying Around

Young monkeys are very active and love to play. They chase each other, wrestle and scamper up and down trees. Two of their favorite games are follow the leader and king of the castle. Sometimes they even tease their mother by swinging on her tail! Luckily for them adult monkeys are usually very patient and will put up with a lot of "monkey business." Playing is not only fun but it helps to make them good climbers and teaches them to get along with others, which is very important in a monkey troop.

Monkeys mature more slowly than other animals their size. The bond between mothers and daughters lasts into adulthood, and females often stay in the troop they were born into. Males, on the other hand, often leave and join other young males in a temporary bachelor group while they wait till they are able to join a new troop.

*Caught in the act!*

## Colorful Coats

In Africa the most common monkeys are the guenons. Most of them live high up in trees, seldom coming down to the ground. The main exceptions are the different types of green monkeys, who nest and take refuge in trees but spend most of their time on the ground.

All guenons have tails longer than their bodies and cheek pouches in which they store food they don't want to eat right away. Guenons are very handsome monkeys about the size of a housecat. Many have brightly colored coats with bold, contrasting patterns. Mustaches, beards and striped sideburns are also common, especially in the males. Their names — red-eared, owl-faced, white-nosed — give you some idea of what they look like. Guenons are quite tolerant of each other and in some areas several different species live happily side by side.

*De Brazza's monkey.*

## Lanky Langurs

Lanky, lean, graceful, these are a few words that describe the langur monkeys of India and parts of the Far East. There are more than 50 different kinds and they come in a variety of sizes, shapes and colors. Some live in forests while others brave the chilly slopes of the Himalaya mountains. They are primarily leaf-eaters and have a special digestive system similar to that of a cow which helps them get as much nourishment as possible from their food.

Most langurs spend the majority of their time in trees. However, the gray or Hanuman langur is mainly a ground dweller. This langur is considered sacred in parts of India and is protected by law, free to roam the countryside and even city streets as it pleases. It is an adaptable monkey that lives in woodlands, forests and farmlands.

*The handsome Hanuman.*

## Super Snout

Meet the Pinocchio of the monkey world, the proboscis monkey. The word proboscis means "long flexible snout" so it's no mystery how this comical-looking monkey got its name. Both the males and the females have long noses but the male's is sometimes so long it hangs below his chin. And the bigger the male's nose is, the more attractive females find him. This super snout is not just there for looks, however; it serves as a loudspeaker when the male gives his loud *honk-keehonk* warning call.

The proboscis monkey is found in swampy forests on the island of Borneo. Leaves make up the bulk of its diet and it spends a good part of the day resting between meals. It can be surprisingly active when it wants to, though. Despite its large size — up to 23 kilograms (52 pounds) for a male — it is an excellent climber. It is also a daring high diver and often jumps from trees into water over 15 metres (50 feet) below — and then dogpaddles away with ease. The proboscis monkey has a nose for trouble and when threatened will dive and swim underwater.

Opposite page: *Rather surprisingly, the super-sized nose of the proboscis monkey does not seem to give it a better sense of smell than other monkeys have.*

## Mangabey Monkeys

Mangabey monkeys live mainly in the forests of West and Central Africa. They come in a variety of colors but all have white upper eyelids that can been seen from great distances. They are slender, long-tailed animals weighing from 3 to 12 kilograms (7 to 26 pounds).

The deep grunting call of the gray-cheeked mangabey sounds like a "hesitant turkey with a frog in its throat." It is a rather noisy monkey that can often be heard high in treetops ripping a meal of bark from trees. It also eats fruit, flowers, insects and birds' eggs, and will bite the head off a snake before eating the rest of it. Gray-cheeked mangabeys have a larger home range than most forest monkeys because they are so effective at finding all available food in an area that they must wait quite a while before returning to it.

*You probably won't be a bit surprised to learn that this mangabey monkey is commonly known as the red-capped mangabey.*

# Royal Family

Most people are familiar with the baboon, the largest of all monkeys. Males can grow to be over a metre (3 feet) tall. Females are about half that size. Baboons are known as dog-faced monkeys. Come to think of it, they do look a bit like a large poodle with their long muzzle. One species, the hamadryas baboon of Ethiopia and Arabia, is the famous sacred monkey of ancient Egypt that was often made into a mummy.

Baboons are ground dwellers and rarely climb trees except to sleep. Troops average about 40 individuals and travel 3 to 4 kilometres (2 to 2.5 miles) a day searching for food. It is believed that some baboons never move more than a metre (3 feet) away from another baboon in their entire life. Now that's togetherness!

Baboons have a reputation for being aggressive and when threatened they can indeed be very ferocious. Male baboons will fight a leopard or even a lion that threatens the troop. However, they are generally friendly and gentle with each other.

Opposite page:
*While the hamadryas baboon can look quite imposing, it is actually the smallest of the baboons.*

## Big Bold and Beautiful

Opposite page: *We still know relatively little about how mandrills live in the wild.*

Let's face it, animals don't get much more colorful than this. With its brilliant blue-ribbed cheeks, red nose and rosy bottom, the mandrill is one of a kind. The males have the brightest colors and when they get angry their face gets even more vivid. Females are not so gaudy and less than half the size of their mates.

Mandrills live in the forests of West Africa and for this reason are known as forest baboons. This is one animal you would not want to "monkey around" with. An adult male is as strong as a leopard and when threatened as powerful as a gorilla. Not to mention the fact that its canine teeth are as long as a tiger's.

Mandrills are big, measuring in at just under a metre (3 feet) tall. Their tails are short for a monkey, usually less than 10 centimetres (4 inches) long. Mandrills walk on their fingers and toes, never letting their palms touch the ground. To rest they often lean forward on their hands. They will eat almost anything, and when water is scarce they dig in the bottom of dry riverbeds to find it.

# Fleet of Foot

If all the primates in the world were to have a race, no one would be able to keep up with the patas monkey. This streamlined, long-legged animal is built like a greyhound. With its bounding gait it can reach speeds of up to 55 kilometres (34 miles) an hour. The patas monkey lives in the savannah regions of Africa. Although it is a ground dweller it will often climb a small tree to find food or to take a quick look around. It also sleeps in trees at night.

The patas monkey belongs to the same family as do the guenons. With its reddish coat and its white mustache, it is a rather dashing looking monkey. Males weigh an average of 10 kilograms (22 pounds) although some may be twice that. Females are smaller, weighing in at about 7 kilograms (15 pounds) or less. A typical troop contains 20 animals or so. Patas monkeys are relatively quiet. Even when threatened they only make soft chirping sounds.

*The patas monkey is also known as the hussar or military monkey.*

# Aerial Acrobats

The colobus monkey has a beautiful coat of long, fine hair. While there are red and olive colobuses, most are a striking black and white.

Colobus monkeys are known as leaf monkeys because they can eat large amounts of foliage. However, some species eat more fruit and seeds than they do leaves. They live in forests in the middle of Africa high up in the treetops. Incredible acrobats, they often leap 8 metres (25 feet) or more from branch to branch. They can even change direction in mid-air! But most of the time they move rather slowly, resting between feedings, and often travel only 500 metres (yards) in a day.

Colobus monkeys are unusual because they only have a small nub of a thumb or none at all. This is how they get their name, which means docked or mutilated. Having no thumbs doesn't slow down these monkeys, though. They are very skilled at picking up things and climbing trees with only their fingers and palms.

## Feeling Frosty

There are more than 15 different species of macaque monkeys in the world. With the exception of one species they all live in Asia. Most have drab brown, gray or yellow coats but some have bright colored skin on their face. Macaques are essentially ground dwellers and are very good at walking on two feet.

Two well-known members of this family are the rhesus monkey, a favorite of zoos, and the Japanese macaque. The Japanese macaque lives the farthest north of all the monkeys in the world. During the winter when snow covers the forests and mountains of Japan and there are no leaves on the trees, these thick-coated animals survive by eating bark. They keep warm by huddling together and by taking dips in nearby hot springs where they dogpaddle in the steaming water.

*Japanese macaque.*

## Helping Out

We owe a great deal to monkeys. Not only are they fascinating to watch, they have helped us in many ways. Thanks to well-trained monkeys many disabled people now have a much needed helper in the home. These faithful companions give their owners an independence never before possible.

Did you know the first astronaut was a rhesus monkey? And that's not its only claim to fame. Thanks to research with these monkeys a vaccine for polio was discovered and many children have been spared from this disabling disease. It was also by studying rhesus monkeys that scientists identified the Rh (for rhesus) positive and negative factors that exist in our blood as well as monkeys'. This too has saved many lives.

Monkeys certainly deserve our respect and protection. It is very important that we stop destroying their forests so that these amazing animals will always have a place to live.

# Special Words

**Canine tooth**   One of four strong pointed teeth, located between the front teeth and the molars.

**Groom**   To clean or brush, especially hair.

**Home range**   Area where an animal lives and looks for food.

**Mate**   To come together to produce young. Either member of an animal pair is also the other's mate.

**Opposable thumb**   The kind of thumb that is separated from the fingers and can be moved around to meet them. Humans and a few animals, including Old World monkeys and chimpanzees, have opposable thumbs.

**Prehensile**   Adapted for grabbing and holding, especially by wrapping around an object. Many New World monkeys and some other animals, such as opossums, have prehensile tails. Old World monkeys, however, do not.

**Primate**   An animal that belongs to the order Primates, such as a monkey, chimpanzee or human being.

**Proboscis**   A long, flexible snout (pronounced pro.BOSS.is).

**Troop**   A group of monkeys that live together. The strongest male is in charge of the troop.

# INDEX

**Cover Photo:**  Bill Ivy
**Photo Credits:**  Bill Ivy, pages 4, 8, 12, 16, 20, 28, 36, 39; George Holton, page 11; Robert Winslow, page 15; Nancy Adams, pages 19, 32, 35, 40; Fletcher & Baylis (Photo Researchers, Inc.), page 22; Brian Vikander (West Light), pages 24, 25; Nancy Staley, page 27; Fred Bavendam (Peter Arnold, Inc.), page 31; Gregory Dimijian (Photo Researchers, Inc.), page 43; Akira Uchiyama (Photo Researchers, Inc.), page 45.